KEEP ME CLEAN

REMEMBER TO WASH YOUR
HANDS BEFORE READING ME

Reconstruction

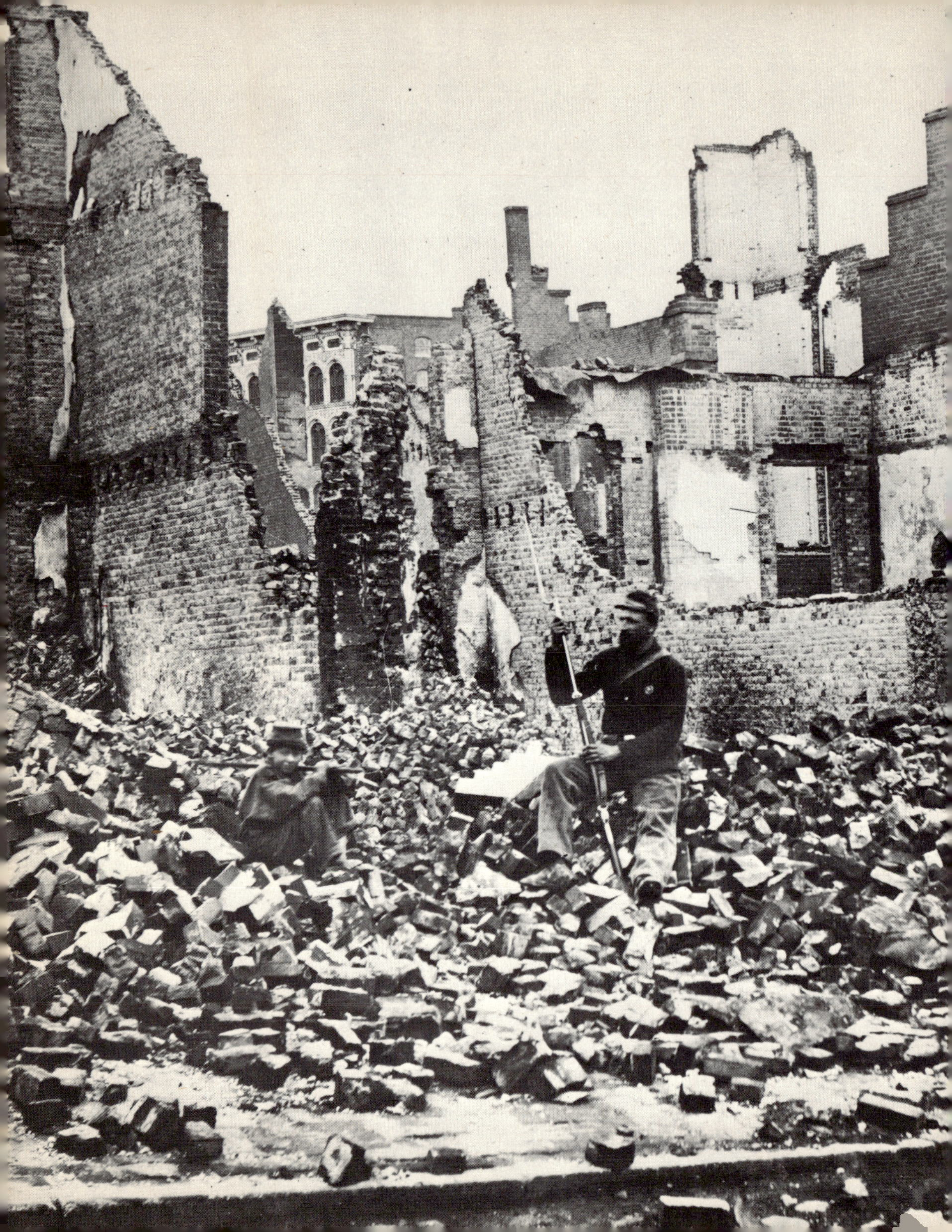

Reconstruction

by Dorothy Levenson

*Illustrated with photographs
and contemporary drawings*

◄─A FIRST BOOK─►

Franklin Watts, Inc.
575 Lexington Avenue
New York, N. Y. 10022

Photographs Courtesy of The Library of Congress

973.8
L
4186

Library of Congress Catalog Card Number: 78-117941
Copyright © 1970 by Franklin Watts, Inc.
Printed in the United States of America
SBN 531-00715-4

1 2 3 4 5

Shrine of the Little Flower School Library
Baltimore, Maryland

Contents

No More	3
The Civil War	3
Black People Before the War	6
Republicans and Democrats	10
Lincoln and Reconstruction	12
The Soldiers Come Home	14
The Walls Come Tumbling Down	20
Forty Acres and a Mule	23
The Freedmen's Bureau	26
Black Churches	29
President Andrew Johnson	30
Radical Republicans	36
Reconstruction Governments	44
Black Representation in Congress	47
Congress and Black Men's Rights	50
Expansion of the North	51
Freedom Road	55
The Election of 1876	58
The End of Reconstruction	62
Index	64

Reconstruction

No More

In 1865, for the first time in the history of the United States, all men were legally free. There were no more slaves.

Until then most white people in the United States had been free and most black people had been slaves. Now all the people of the United States — black and white — were free in the eyes of the law. For twelve years, from 1865 to 1877, black and white men tried to rebuild their nation, to make it a country where all men could live together in freedom. This is the story of how they tried and failed.

The Civil War

From 1861 to 1865, for four long years, the people of the United States fought among themselves. These were the years of the Civil War, when the North fought the South. Armies of American soldiers marched up and down American roads, burning houses and barns, tearing up railroads, and blowing up trains. American soldiers killed other American soldiers, and by the time the war ended, hundreds of thousands of men had died.

When it was all over, there were many Americans who hated great numbers of other Americans, their countrymen. Women whose husbands and sons had been killed hated the men who had

Wounded soldiers waited to go home.

done the killing. Men who had spent months ill and suffering in hospitals and prisons hated the men who had kept them there.

Northerners hated Southerners, whom they blamed for starting the war. Southerners hated Northerners — the "damned Yankees" — who had burned their cities and farms.

The Northern states and the Southern states had argued for many years before the war began. They argued about slavery and they argued about the kinds of laws and taxes that were best for the country. In 1861, eleven Southern states — Alabama, Arkansas, Florida, Georgia, Louisiana, Mississippi, North Carolina, South Carolina, Tennessee, Texas, and Virginia — decided that they would no longer be part of the United States. Together they set up a separate country and chose Jefferson Davis to be their president. They named their new country the Confederate States of America.

The people of the Confederacy wanted to be independent. The United States, under President Abraham Lincoln, wanted to "preserve the Union" — to keep all the states together as one country. So the two nations went to war. The Confederacy had only 8,700,000 people, of which three and a half million were black. The North had 22,700,000 people. In addition, the North had more money, more factories to make guns, more railroads, more of all the things needed to make war.

The North won. Union armies marched south and defeated the Confederacy. By April, 1865, Southern soldiers, unable to fight any more, surrendered.

The war was over. Now came the problem of Reconstruction,

Jefferson Davis, president of the Confederacy.

of rebuilding the United States as one country. For twelve years the government in Washington tried to rebuild the nation. Even more important, the people of the United States — North and South, black and white — struggled to rebuild their nation.

Houses that had been burned had to be rebuilt. New cities had to be built in the ruins of the old. Above all, the nation had to be rebuilt as a whole. There was no more Condeferacy. The United States was one country again. These Northerners and Southerners who hated each other had to learn to live together again.

And all the people, North and South, had to learn to live with the black people who had been slaves and now were free. White men and black men had to learn to live together as free citizens of the United States.

Black People Before the War

Before the Civil War, 3,500,000 black people in the United States were slaves. A slave belonged to the man who owned him, the way a horse or a dog belongs to a man. A slave had to work for the man who owned him, but at any time he could be sold to a new master. Women and children were slaves too. A slave child could be separated from his parents, sold, and taken away so that he never saw his family again.

Most black slaves lived in the Southern states. The majority belonged to the men who owned the great farms of the South — the cotton and tobacco plantations. Some of them worked in the fields. Some of them worked in the great houses, cleaning and polishing, and taking care of the children. A few lived in cities. But wherever they were and whatever they did, most black men were slaves. They belonged to masters who decided what kind of work they should do and who punished them if they felt they did not work hard enough.

Before the Civil War, there were about 500,000 black people in the United States who were not slaves. Some had bought their freedom, some had run away from their masters. Sometimes a master freed his slaves. But to be a "free" black man was not the same as to be a free white man. Free black men in the South had to be very careful. There were all kinds of extra rules for them them to follow. They could not travel without a special pass and often they had to be in their houses by a certain time each day.

Even in the North it was not easy to be free and black. Most states did not allow black men to vote. In many places they were not allowed to give evidence against a white man. If a black man was robbed by a white man the black man could not say so in front of a judge. If he was beaten by a white man the black man could not tell a jury. Some states did not want black people to live within their borders at all. Illinois, Indiana, and Oregon had laws that said black people could not come to live in those states.

Most people in the North, however, did think that slavery was wrong. As the war went on, more and more people in the North came to believe that slaves should be freed.

Freedom came slowly. In January of 1863, Abraham Lincoln signed his Emancipation Proclamation. It said that all the slaves in the rebel states were free; however, it said nothing about slaves in those parts of the country controlled by the Union army. In

After the Emancipation Proclamation many black slaves ran away to the protection of the Northern army.

fact, the proclamation did not actually free a single slave. But to most people it came as a promise that one day all the slaves would be free. There was celebration in many places. In Boston, people listened to the words of a poet:

> I break your bonds and masterships,
> And I unchain the slave;
> Free be his heart and hand thenceforth
> As wind and wandering wave.

When black men joined the Northern army to fight for freedom for their people, the news spread all over the South. Slaves had always had ways of passing along news that concerned them. On many lonely plantations slaves stopped work and sang their songs:

>No more auction block for me,
>No more, no more,
>No more auction block for me:
>Many thousand gone.

>No more driver's lash for me,
>No more, no more,
>No more driver's lash for me;
>Many thousand gone.

Many slaves left their plantations and followed Lincoln's troops. When the war ended in victory for the North most people North and South accepted this as the end of slavery.

But most white men, North and South, were not ready to accept black men as equal citizens. White Southerners were worried because in some states there were more black people than white people.

Even Abraham Lincoln had not decided what to do with the slaves once they were free. He thought of sending them all back to Africa. He asked one of his generals to figure out how it could be done. But four million black mothers and fathers and children were too many to pack on ships. Lincoln's general reported back to him that black people could not be shipped to Africa "half as fast as Negro children will be born here."

Black men knew what they wanted. For many years free black men and women in the North had worked to help slaves in the South. Frederick Douglass had been born a slave. When he grew up, he disguised himself in sailor's clothes, borrowed a pass from a free black, and ran away. He came north, where he met other men — black and white — who were fighting against slavery. Frederick Douglass spoke at meetings and even traveled to England to talk about slavery to people there. He bought a newspaper so that he could write and publish the story of slavery.

When the war came, Douglass went to President Lincoln to tell him that black men wanted to fight. After the war he knew what the white man should do with the black man. He said: "Let him alone; he has a right to work. If you see him on his way to school . . . let him alone. If he has a ballot in his hand . . . let him alone."

The answer was not so simple to white men. In both the North and the South they were to go on arguing about what it meant to be a free black man.

Republicans and Democrats

The Civil War destroyed many things in the United States. But it did not destroy the two great political parties: the Republican party and the Democratic party.

Abraham Lincoln and the Republican party had led the people of the North through the war. The Democratic party was the party of the South — the leaders of the Confederacy had all been Democrats. However, there were still Democrats in the North, and throughout the war the Democratic party continued to exist there.

Frederick Douglass.

After the war the debate about Reconstruction went on all over the country, but it was especially hot in Washington and in the Southern states. It was Republicans and Democrats who debated. The farmers and factory owners of the North supported the Republican party, and black men, in both the North and the South, voted Republican. Most of the white men of the South were Democrats, but many poor men of the Northern cities also began to vote Democratic.

Republicans and Democrats argued in Congress about how to treat black people and how to treat the South. Some people felt that the leaders of the Confederacy should be punished. During the war there had been a popular song that said: "We're gonna hang Jeff Davis on a sour apple tree."

This did not happen. Davis was arrested and held in prison for two years. Then he was released.

Lincoln and Reconstruction

Lincoln was president of the United States all through the Civil War. He had many quarrels with people inside and outside of Congress about how the South should be treated when the war was over. One of the disputes was about whether the Southern states had really left the Union. Was the Confederacy a separate country? Lincoln said no. He declared that the people of the Southern states were in rebellion, but the states had not left the United States. There could be no real problem about their coming back in. Other people said those Southern states had left and should be treated as a foreign country.

Lincoln was a strong president and was able to win most of his arguments with Congress. As the Union armies marched south Lincoln took charge. As the states were reconquered he appointed military governors to rule them. In 1862 and 1863 he sent military governors to Tennessee, Arkansas, and Louisiana.

Late in 1863 Lincoln announced his plan for Reconstruction. The leaders of the Confederacy would not be allowed to vote. Almost every other Southerner would have a chance to take an oath saying that he was loyal to the United States. As soon as ten percent of the voters in any state had taken that oath the state could come back into the Union.

This plan made many congressmen angry. Some were angry because they felt the South should be punished for going to war. Others wanted to make sure that black men were really free — Lincoln had said nothing about giving the vote to them.

Lincoln and Congress continued to argue. Congress passed a bill that would have made it much more difficult for a state to come back. Lincoln vetoed, or said no to, that bill, and the debate went on — for as long as Lincoln lived.

On March 4, 1865, Lincoln stood on the Capitol steps in Washington. He was to be sworn in as president of the United States for the second time. It was a cold, dreary, windy day. There had been rain, the streets were muddy, and the wide skirts of the women on hand dragged in the mud. But it was a hopeful time. The war was almost over. Lincoln knew that and he spoke of what had to be done next. He knew how much hatred there was in the country. He knew about the homes and barns that had been destroyed. He knew how important it was to end slavery.

Lincoln said that when the war began "one eighth of the whole population were colored slaves." He hoped that the war was almost over. "Yet, if God wills that it continue until all the wealth piled up by the bondsman's two hundred and fifty years of unrequited toil shall be sunk, and until every drop of blood drawn with the lash shall be paid by another drawn with the sword," the war must go on.

Lincoln knew that once the war was over the next step would be to "bind up the nation's wounds" and to make one country again out of the North and South.

The crowd listened to Lincoln. There were soldiers in the crowd who had suffered on the battlefields. There were many black people there that day listening in hope.

Also listening was Andrew Johnson, the vice-president, who was from Tennessee. Although he was trying to, Johnson was not listening too closely, because he had drunk too much whiskey in an attempt to cure a bad case of flu.

Andrew Johnson, not Lincoln, would guide the country through the first difficult years of Reconstruction. Six weeks after the ceremony on the Capitol steps. Lincoln was dead. On April 14, he had

President Andrew Johnson.

gone to the theater with Mrs. Lincoln and as he sat watching the play he was shot. That shot, which killed Lincoln the next day, added to the anger that already filled the country, and it made Andrew Johnson president.

The Soldiers Come Home

Peace came to the whole country in that spring of 1865. Soldiers from both armies hurried home to their families. Many of them came from farms and wanted to be home in time for the spring plowing. Yankee soldiers returned home to a land that was prosperous. Most of their families had come through the war safely.

A Yankee soldier comes home.

Southern soldiers, however, went back to ruins. Almost all the battles of the Civil War were fought in the South. Farmhouses and barns were burned. Fields were torn up by guns. Thousands of people had run away from the advancing armies. In the last months of the war Northern soldiers destroyed as much of the South as possible. Northern soldiers set fire to farms and cities. They stole cows and chickens to eat because they were hungry. They killed the ones they could not eat so that Southern soldiers would go hungry. Great cities of the South were in ruins. Many sections of Richmond, Virginia; Atlanta, Georgia; and Columbia, South Carolina, were nothing but rubble.

Southern cities lay in ruins.

Black soldiers hurried home to be with their families.

People were traveling all over the South that spring. Soldiers were coming home from the army. Former slaves were wandering the roads looking for work or a place to live. During the war thousands of people had left their homes. When a battle was being fought on a man's farm it was safer to go somewhere else. Now families were coming back to their old homes.

Many Northerners were coming south. The South was a conquered land. Soldiers and government officials were coming south to rule. Some Northerners — both white and black — were coming south to help those who had suffered during the war. Teachers and doctors came to set up schools and hospitals. Some Northerners came because they thought the South might be a good place to make money. Newspapers and magazines sent reporters to write stories. Some politicians came to look at the South themselves; some sent other men to make reports.

Travel was hard for all these people. The South had not had good roads before the war. In rainy weather the dirt roads there turned to mud. In swampy places logs were sometimes laid across the road to help. For four years no one had had time to take care of the roads. Now it was so hard to find one where a wagon or a carriage could pass that riding horseback or walking was the best way to get around.

The railroads were in worse shape. The locomotives were old and rusty, and the Northerners had done their best to wreck the railroads. Soldiers had torn up tracks, blown up bridges, and smashed locomotives. Riding a railroad anywhere in the South in 1865 was an adventure. Trains broke down because they needed new parts. Passengers often had to leave a train when they came to a river because the bridge was no longer there. They had to cross the river in boats and pick up another train on the other side.

There were not many good roads in the South. Mules were the most common animals used for hauling.

Railroad bridges had been destroyed.

There was no food to be had on the trains. When a train stopped at little country towns, there would be a crowd waiting to sell food to the passengers — fruit, corn bread, chicken, or eggs.

Soldiers coming home rode trains when they could, rode horses if they had them, or walked on tired, sore feet.

No Southern soldier knew what he would find when he reached home. If he came from a city he might find his house just a pile of broken bricks. If he was a poor farmer he might find his farm had been sold because his wife could not keep up with the work while he was away. If he was a rich plantation owner he might find his beautiful house burned or all its furniture chopped up to make wood for Yankee campfires. Often a soldier could find no trace of his family. If he did find them they might be as ill and hungry as he was himself.

Many Southern soldiers came back to find their homes in ruins.

There was no government in the South to help. Jefferson Davis was in prison. Northern military governors tried, but they did not have large enough staffs. There was no one to help the soldiers find their families. No one to pay them. No one to run the post office so that people could write to each other. No one to start rebuilding the cities.

Strangest of all there was no money. The Confederate government had printed its own money. Now that there was no more Confederacy, Confederate money was not worth anything. Housewives found they could not buy food for their families. Workmen found their wages were not worth anything. Many men found they had nothing left but a piece of land and no one had any money to buy that from them.

The greatest change the Southern soldier found when he came home was that there were no more slaves. Before the war there had been two kinds of men in the South: white men who were free and black men who were slaves. Now all men were legally free.

The Walls Come Tumbling Down

Millions of black people were suddenly free. Other travelers were surprised to find the roads full of former slaves. Where were they going? Many were just wandering — enjoying the fact that they could walk wherever they wanted. Plantations had been their prisons. Many ex-slaves wanted to get up and go as far away from those prisons as possible.

All over the South black people wandered the roads.

Many were setting out to look for their families. All over the South slavery had scattered black families far and wide. Once they were free, husbands set out to look for wives, and parents and children sought each other.

The first thing many black men and women did when they became free was to be married by a real clergyman. They wanted to be married and to know that no one could separate them. The certificate given when they were married was a treasured document that was framed and hung on the living room wall for everyone to see. Black women wanted a wedding ring — a gold wedding ring.

THE STATE OF	COUNTY OF
South Carolina	Richland

Under the Protection of Almighty God.
Marriage Certificate.

KNOW ALL MEN BY THESE PRESENTS,

That I, *W. D. Harris*, have this, the *Fifth (5)* day of *October* 1870, joined together in HOLY WEDLOCK, *Abel Pinckney* and *Amelia McMillan* in conformity with the laws of this State.

In Witness whereof, I have hereunto set my hand and seal.

WITNESSES:
Congregation at the Bethel A.M.E. Church Columbia, S.C.

W. D. Harris
Minister
[L.S.]

J. W. Denny, Printer, Columbia, S.C.

A marriage certificate issued to Abel Pinckney and Amelia McMillan, two former slaves, in 1870. Instead of only two witnesses signing the certificate, the whole "congregation at the Bethel A.M.E. Church, Columbia, South Carolina," stood witness to the wedding.

Often they could not get enough money together to pay for a ring all at once. Peddlers came around selling rings, and the women bought them, paying the peddler a quarter a week until the ring was paid for.

Most slaves had only one name — Mary or Tom or Betty. Now they could have two names — and many families spent a long time deciding what their second name should be.

Forty Acres and a Mule

Many black people were roaming the roads looking for a place to live and some way to make a living.

Freedom — legal freedom — was the only thing the slaves were given. Slaves owned nothing — no money, no land, no houses, no cows, no mules. Everything had belonged to the master. Slaves did not even own the clothes they wore.

The freedmen had nothing with which to start a new life. Few of them could read or write because it had been against the law in most parts of the South to educate a slave. Most black men could not read about this strange new world in which they found themselves.

There was talk that when the slaves were freed Mr. Lincoln would give each man forty acres and a mule. Black men dreamed of owning their own land — farming was the business that they knew best. There was more to this dream. This was still a time in the

United States when a man who owned his own piece of land could be independent. All over the country were small farms where a family could grow all that it needed.

A farmer grew his own fruits and vegetables. His wife dried and preserved them for the winter. A cow gave the family milk and cream, which could be made into butter and cheese. There was plenty of good hunting — enough deer or rabbits or wild turkeys to keep a farmer's family in meat. The farmer's wife made almost all that the family needed — clothes and soap and candles. A hard-working family on its own piece of land need not answer to anyone.

Before the war there had been two kinds of farms in the South. There were small farms worked by the farmer and his famly. There were big plantations worked by large groups of slaves. After the war ex-slaves, who had no money, hoped that they would be given land so that they could become small farmers. Here and there ex-slaves tried to take over a plantation for themselves. Here and there an army officer helped them. But there was no legal way to get land without money.

The Homestead Act had been passed in May, 1862. It gave to "any person who is the head of a family or who has arrived at the age of twenty-one years, and is a citizen of the United States, or who shall have filed his declaration of intention to become such," the right to 160 acres of land free (except for a small fee for filing his claim). All the farmer had to do was to live on his land and farm it for five years.

The freedmen could not afford this "free" land. Most of the available land was out west. To go homesteading a man needed enough money to pay railroad fares for himself and his family. He had to buy a plow and seed. He had to be able to feed his family until a crop came in. Ex-slaves did not have enough money for all that. Besides, there was usually nobody around to tell them about the Homestead Act.

Northern cities did not welcome black people. Poor white immigrants from Europe worked in the factories and mines of the North. They were afraid that black men might take their jobs. The only way many ex-slaves could make a living was to go back to work on the old plantation.

In the years before the war when men had talked about doing away with slavery they had often talked about "compensation." Many men believed that the master should be paid something for the slaves who were freed. When freedom came at the end of the long war, men were bitter, and freeing the slaves was seen as a way of punishing the South. Lincoln still talked of compensation, but Congress would not hear of it. When the slaves were freed their owners were not paid anything. This was a punishment for all the South, for the South needed money with which to rebuild its farms and cities. Plantation owners needed money to pay wages to the freedmen. Rich men in the North had invested their money in factories and railroads. Rich men in the South had invested their money in slaves. They had lost their slaves and lost their money.

Ex-slaves had no money — and neither did the plantation owners. The ex-slaves wanted to work — and the farmers needed men to work for them. Farmers needed money for other things — to buy stock and fertilizer. Farm buildings needed repairs.

Freedmen and farmers had to find a way to start farming without money. Sharecropping was often the answer. Freedmen and owners agreed to work the land together and to split the crop at the end of the year. A sharecropper was given a house, fuel, and food in return for part of his crop. If both owner and sharecropper were honest, this could work. But there were many arguments between the plantation owners and the freedmen. Somehow the sharecropper always seemed to end up with very little for his year's work. The owner was so worried about paying back the money he had borrowed from the bank to buy seed that he did not have much sympathy for the sharecropper.

The Freedmen's Bureau

All the people of the South, black and white, needed help. The federal government set up the Bureau of Refugees, Freedmen and Abandoned Lands. Officers of the bureau went to work all over the South trying to help whoever needed aid. In four years, 21,000,000 rations of food were handed out. Three-quarters of the food went to black families, but the rest went to hungry white men, women, and children. Even before the war the South had not had enough doctors and hospitals. Now there were thousands of sick and wounded soldiers. In two years the bureau set up forty-six hospitals with their own doctors and nurses.

The bureau helped the freedmen by explaining the new way of life to them and to white men. Often a white man found it hard to understand that he could no longer hit a black man who argued with him or did not want to work for him. When white farmers and black workers could not agree about wages they came to an officer of the Freedmen's Bureau to settle matters. Black men often did not feel safe in local courts run by white men, so the bureau set up freedmen's courts.

White Southerners came to the Freedmen's Bureau for food.

Five million dollars were spent by the bureau setting up schools for ex-slaves. There were many different kinds of schools — from elementary schools to colleges. Northern teachers — both white and black — came south to teach in schools that were open during the day, at night, and on Sundays. Black children came to school — and so did their mothers and fathers, even grandmothers and grandfathers. Before the war only white men had been allowed to read and write. Now black families saw education as the way to complete freedom.

Black children in school for the first time.

Many white people also saw schools as the best way to help. Wealthy men gave money, and both white and black churches helped to start colleges.

The students themselves helped. At Hampton Institute in Virginia the students did all the work — the cooking and the cleaning and the building. The students at Fisk University in Nashville, Tennessee, knew that their school needed more money. They formed a choir — the Fisk Jubilee Singers — and traveled all over the world giving concerts. The money they made was sent back to the university.

Black Churches

Just as they wanted schools, black people wanted churches. Black people were not welcome in most white churches, in either the North or the South. Free black men had formed their own churches in the North before the Civil War. After the war they were able to organize their own churches in the South.

There was not much money to build churches or to pay ministers. A black bishop was paid less than two hundred dollars a year. But there were hundreds of thousands of black people eager to join a church. The African Methodist Episcopal Church had ten times as many members in 1876 as it had in 1856. By 1870, there were 500,000 black people worshiping in their own Baptist churches.

Now the black people of the South could have their own weddings and funerals and christenings. On Sundays they could all gather together to pray and sing.

Many of the ministers were not well-educated. Some of them had just learned to read and write themselves. Their salaries were so low that often they had to be farmers all week or hold other jobs to support their families. But they understood the people in their churches. They had been slaves themselves, so they knew how hard freedom could be.

Most black men did not own farms or businesses of their own. Most had to work for white men. Even the men who ran the black colleges found they had to be polite to the white men who gave them money. The churches, however, belonged to the black people who built them and sang in them.

President Andrew Johnson

While black and white people in the South struggled to find a way to live in the new freedom, politicians in Washington talked. President Lincoln was dead, and President Johnson was planning for the South.

Abraham Lincoln and Andrew Johnson both had been born in log cabins. Johnson was born in Raleigh, North Carolina, where his father's job was to sweep and clean the bank there. When he was ten years old Andrew was sent to live with a tailor so that he could learn to be a tailor himself.

Little Andrew Johnson worked hard all through his childhood. Abraham Lincoln worked hard too, but that was on the family farm with his father and brothers and sisters. Andrew Johnson worked for a stranger. He had no chance to go to school or play games or do any of the things a boy should do. The tailor was cruel, and he beat Andrew. As soon as the boy was old enough, he ran away to Tennessee and became a tailor himself. Tailor Johnson wanted to learn but he had not gone to school and he could not read. That did not stop him. There were men around who could read. Johnson paid them fifty cents an hour to read to him while he stitched. When he married, his wife read to him at night while he cut and sewed clothes for other people. At last his wife taught him to read and write for himself.

Johnson became interested in politics. The friends he gathered around him in the tailor shop helped elect him to city council. He became a state legislator, a congressman, and then governor of Tennessee. Tailor Johnson went off to Washington as a senator. He belonged to the Democratic party, as did most of the people in the

Andrew Johnson's tailor shop.

Mrs. Andrew Johnson. She taught her husband to read and write.

South. Johnson did not always agree with other Southern Democrats. Many of them were rich slave owners and Johnson never forgot how poor he had been. His sympathy was with the small farmers and little shopkeepers of Southern towns. He was not interested in fighting a war to help slave owners.

When the Civil War began, all the other congressmen from Tennessee went home to help the Confederacy. Andrew Johnson was loyal to the Union. He thought Tennessee should remain part of the United States, so he stayed in Washington and worked for peace. Abraham Lincoln thought of him as a true friend. In 1862, when Tennessee was captured by Union troops, Lincoln made Johnson military governor of Tennessee.

Johnson's loyalty to the Union made him president. In 1864, when Lincoln had to run for reelection, the war was not going well. Men in the Republican party who were afraid that Lincoln might be defeated thought that the votes of people who were sympathetic to the South might be important. The politicians looked around for a loyal Southerner — and found Andrew Johnson. He was chosen to run as Lincoln's vice-president. When Lincoln was killed, Johnson became president.

The little tailor was a stubborn man and a brave one. When he thought he was right he could stand up to anyone. He had the same kind of courage when he became president. He was ready to battle all of Congress when he thought he was right and they were wrong.

Johnson proved that he was sympathetic to the South. He quickly allowed the white people of most Southern states to set up their own governments. Because he had been a poor man he did not like rich men; and the only people he did not allow to vote were those men who had $20,000 worth of property or more, and some officials in the Confederate army and government.

During 1865 and 1866 the white people of the South began to govern their own states again. Their first problem was to make up their minds about the former slaves. They knew that the North had won the war. That meant the end of slavery. They ratified the Thirteenth Amendment to the Constitution, which said that there should be no more slaves in the United States. But they still felt black people had to be controlled. Most of these new Southern governments passed laws which meant that black people, if they were not slaves, were not exactly free either. The laws — called Black Codes — said that black men had to work whether they wanted to or not. If a black man quit his job he could be arrested and put in jail. Black men were not allowed to give evidence against a white man in court. They were not allowed to vote. They could be imprisoned or fined if they argued against the laws or insulted a white man. They could be put in jail if they were not at home by a certain hour every night or if they owned guns.

Many Southerners did not wait for the laws to be passed. Stories of the ill-treatment of ex-slaves came to Washington. President Johnson sent one of his generals to the South to find out what was happening. The general, horrified, wrote to the president: "Some planters held back their former slaves on their plantations by brute force. Armed bands of white men patrolled the country roads to drive back the Negroes wandering about. Dead bodies of murdered Negroes were found on and near the highways and byways. Gruesome reports came from the hospitals — reports of colored men and women whose ears had been cut off, whose skulls had been broken by blows, whose bodies had been slashed by knives. . . . A reign of terror prevailed in many parts of the South."

In Memphis, Tennessee, there was a riot in which forty-six blacks were killed. A large number were killed in New Orleans. Black

Whites and blacks battled in Memphis, Tennessee, in May, 1866. Forty-six black people, including many who had been Union soldiers, were killed. Seventy-five were wounded.

people were terrified. Was this freedom? White people in the North were angry. Was it for this they had fought a long war?

In December, 1865, Congress met in Washington. Congressmen from the North looked at the men who had been elected from the South. There was the man who had been vice-president of the Confederacy. There stood four Confederate generals, five Confederate colonels, six Confederate cabinet officers, and fifty-eight members of the Confederate Congress.

The Republicans in Congress were angry with the South and angry with President Johnson for allowing loyal Confederates to serve in the United States government so soon after the war.

Whites and blacks also fought in New Orleans in 1866. Thirty-five black people were killed. A cartoonist showed President Johnson as a Roman emperor watching people being killed in the arena.

A new kind of war broke out. It was a war of words and not of guns, war between President Johnson and his Congress. Presidents and congresses have often disagreed but never so fiercely as in those days after the Civil War.

Congress refused to seat the senators and representatives elected under the Johnson plan. Instead, a Joint Committee on Reconstruction was set up by the Senate and the House of Representatives. As long as Johnson was president, he and Congress fought. The Republican party controlled Congress but some Republicans felt more strongly than others about the South and about freedom for everyone. They were called Radical Republicans.

Radical Republicans

Thaddeus Stevens, the leader of the Radical Republicans, was an old man of seventy-three when the war ended. He had been fighting to free black people for many years and he was not about to stop now.

He was a fierce old man with flashing dark eyes and a thick black wig to hide his bald head. Thaddeus had been very bitter all his life. He was born in a little village in Vermont — and born with a clubfoot. Perhaps it was his foot that made him bitter. The crippled boy who braved the ice and snow to the local schoolhouse was often cold and hungry. His father had left his mother and she had to bring up the children alone. Thaddeus struggled on to go to college and become a lawyer.

He moved to Pennsylvania. The land was softer than cold Vermont, but his early years had given him great sympathy for people in trouble. For many years before the Civil War he fought hard to free the slaves. After the war he understood that freedom was not enough. He fought for laws to protect black men and to give them land.

Thaddeus had an ability to hate. "I could cut his damn heart out," or "Damn him, he ought to hang," were the kinds of things he said about other politicians.

He had a fierce humor too. Once, when a lady admirer asked him for a lock of his hair, Thaddeus took off his wig and handed it to her. As he lay dying a friend came to call. The friend said he was worried about Thad's appearance. Thad could still joke. "It is not my appearance but my disappearance that troubles me," he said.

Thaddeus Stevens died in 1868. In Pennsylvania in those days

A newspaper cartoonist showed President Andrew Johnson and Thaddeus Stevens, leader of the Radical Republicans in Congress, as rival engineers on a collision course.

Thaddeus Stevens, fierce fighter for land and freedom for black people.

most towns had separate graveyards for white people and black people. Stevens did not want to be buried where his black friends were not allowed. He bought a piece of land in a black cemetery so that he could be buried there. On the stone at the head of his grave were carved the words he had written:

> I repose in this quiet and secluded spot
> not from any natural preference for solitude,
> but finding other cemeteries
> limited by charter rules as to race,
> I have chosen this that I might illustrate in my death
> The Principles which I have advocated through a long life:
> Equality of Man Before His Creator.

There were other strong men in Congress. Charles Sumner of Massachusetts was slim, well-dressed, always a gentleman. He too had fought against slavery for many years. Once, when he was

Charles Sumner from Massachusetts.  "Bluff Ben" Wade from Ohio.*

sitting in his office, he had been attacked by a Southern congressman with a walking stick. Sumner was so badly beaten that he was ill for many years afterward.

"Bluff Ben" Wade from Ohio was a rough, tough man of the frontier. He had the rough, tough humor of the West. Dueling had always been popular in the South. When a gentleman felt that he or his family had been insulted by someone, he was likely to challenge that person to a duel. The two gentlemen would meet for a match — usually with pistols — and one of them might be killed. Northerners thought dueling rather silly and they did not quite know what to do when challenged to a duel. Ben Wade knew what to do. When an angry Southerner wanted to fight him, Ben claimed that he had the choice of weapons and he chose "turkey rifles at ten paces." The Southerner did not know if Ben was bluffing. But it sounded too dangerous to find out. After that, Senator Wade was always known as "Bluff Ben" Wade.

Men like these were determined to make sure that black men were to be truly free and that the South was "reconstructed."

In April, 1866, Congress passed a civil rights bill that allowed black men to vote and said that they must have equal rights before the law. President Johnson still held Southern views and tried to veto the bill. Congress outvoted him.

The same month the Joint Committee on Reconstruction asked Congress to pass the Fourteenth Amendment to the Constitution, which said that anyone born or naturalized in the United States was a citizen. Confederate officers were barred from holding office. The Confederate debt was repudiated; no one was going to pay back the money that the Confederate government had borrowed.

It was an election year for Congress in 1866. The debate about the South went on all over the country. Senators and representatives went back home to tell the voters what had been going on in Washington. Although President Johnson did not have to run for reelection that year, he decided that he wanted to tell his story to the voters too.

Until Johnson, no president had done much traveling. Very few people in the country had ever seen a president. In the days of horse-drawn coaches, traveling was too slow and difficult. No one expected presidents to go around from town to town making speeches and meeting people. Andrew Johnson changed all that. He realized that trains made travel much easier and quicker. Off he went by train to Chicago and other midwestern cities.

The speaking tour was not a success. Many people found the very idea of a president traveling and making speeches to all these crowds undignified. They were shocked when noisy people at open-air meetings shouted at the president. They were even more shocked when the president shouted right back.

The president's political experience had been in Tennessee. He was used to audiences of rough backwoodsmen, but the style that suited them did not suit people in Chicago. Johnson was a Southerner, and the crowds were Northern. Many men there were ex-soldiers not long back from the war; many others had lost friends or fathers or husbands in that war. They did not like Johnson's Southern accent.

Newspapers made fun of Johnson and audiences heckled him.

Newspaper cartoonists were not polite to a president they did not like. Johnson is shown making a deal with the Confederate States of America (C.S.A.), shown as a devil.

He did not do much to help the congressmen he wanted elected. When the votes came in that November the Radical Republicans were in control of Congress.

All through 1867 Congress was busy passing laws to make the South over the way the Radical Republicans wanted. Johnson's own state of Tennessee had ratified the Fourteenth Amendment and had come back into the Union. The ten other Southern states were divided into five military districts with a major general in charge of each. Each state elected a constitutional convention. Blacks and loyal whites voted for the conventions, which drew up a new constitution for each state. Congress read and approved these constitutions. After each state ratified the Fourteenth Amendment an election was held. Each state was allowed to ask to come back into the Union.

Johnson tried to veto all these laws, but Congress was able to outvote him. Many men in Congress were so angry with Johnson that they wanted to get rid of him as president. An American president is elected for four years. The only way to remove him before the end of his four-year term, and the time of another election, is to impeach him. Under the Constitution, the House of Representatives can accuse a president of wrongdoing; then he is tried by the Senate. Two thirds of the senators present must vote against a president to convict him.

Andrew Johnson is the only president who has ever been tried — and he was almost convicted. Congress had passed a law to keep a man they preferred as Johnson's secretary of war. Johnson did not like that particular man and so he fired him. Congress then accused Johnson of breaking the law and brought him up for trial before the Senate. When the senators voted they found Johnson guilty; but the vote was thirty-five to nineteen. That was not enough.

Thirty-six votes would have made two thirds — Johnson was saved by one vote.

Johnson was still president, but the speaking tour and the impeachment showed how unpopular he was. The Republicans did not want him again. They wanted someone who would be tough with the South. When the time came to choose another candidate they nominated Ulysses S. Grant, the greatest of Northern generals during the Civil War. Grant was elected president in 1868 and again in 1872.

So many people wanted to see President Johnson's trial that tickets were issued as if it were a show.

President Ulysses S. Grant.

Reconstruction Governments

The Southern states reorganized their governments under the new rules. By 1868, Arkansas, North Carolina, South Carolina, Florida, Alabama, and Louisiana came back into the Union. In 1870, Virginia, Georgia, Mississippi, and Texas were readmitted. Now all the states that had left the Union and set up the Confederacy had returned. The United States was whole again. No state has left since.

What kinds of governments were these? They were like no other governments that had ever been seen in the South. They were governments in which white and black men worked together.

Men rubbed their eyes in amazement as they looked around. There was a black lieutenant governor in Louisiana. In Washington there were black men in the Senate and the House of Representatives. All over the South there were black men in positions of power: black mayors, black postmasters, black policemen, black lawyers, and black judges.

No one should have been surprised that once blacks could vote they would rise to positions of power. In some Southern states there were more black people than whites. In South Carolina there were 291,000 whites and 412,000 blacks. In Mississippi there were 353,000 whites and 437,000 blacks. In several other states there were almost as many blacks as whites.

White men and black men found they could work together in government, go to school together, ride streetcars together, sit down and eat together.

None of this was easy. When Pinckney Benton Stewart Pinchback, a black man, was serving as acting governor of Louisiana,

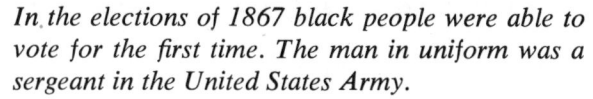

In the elections of 1867 black people were able to vote for the first time. The man in uniform was a sergeant in the United States Army.

Pinckney Benton Stewart Pinchback, black governor of Louisiana during Reconstruction.

police had to escort his children to school to keep them safe from street mobs.

These Reconstruction governments were the most democratic the South had ever known. Before the war only rich men had voted. Now the poor white farmers of the Southern mountains could vote. Many of these farmers had never liked the war. They thought of it as a "rich man's war and a poor man's fight." Now they had their chance. They became part of these new governments.

These men set about giving the South some of the things that had not existed before the war. There were few public schools in the South, and only the rich could afford private schools or tutors to educate their children. In addition to the numbers of ex-slaves

There were many poor white farmers in the mountains of the South.

This was the great age of railroads.

who could not read or write, there were thousands of white m
who had never been to school. The states began setting up pub
school systems. There had never been enough roads or railroa
and help was now given to companies that wanted to come in and
build.

Neither the white nor the black legislators had much experience. Many mistakes were made. In these postwar years there were many dishonest politicians in both the North and South. Many made themselves rich by passing the laws that they or their friends wanted.

Many Northerners came south. Some came to help, but others came to get what they could for themselves. They were called "carpetbaggers" because they often carried their possessions in soft bags made from carpeting.

Black Representation in Congress

Through these years of Reconstruction black men were elected to Congress. In the early 1870's six black men sat in the House of Representatives in Washington and one black man served in the Senate. Altogether, from the end of the Civil War to the end of the nineteenth century, two black senators and twenty black representatives were elected.

What kind of men were these black congressmen? Many of them had been freedmen in either the North or the South before the war.

The first black members of Congress.

All of them had had some education — some of them a great deal. Ten had been to college, five were lawyers.

Hiram R. Revels took over Jefferson Davis' old seat in the Senate. His parents had been free blacks in North Carolina before the war. When Revels went to Washington to take his seat in the Senate some Democrats tried to stop him. They quoted the law which said a United States senator had to have been a United States citizen before the war. They maintained that since Revels was black he could not have been a citizen for a long enough time.

Blanche K. Bruce was the only black man to serve a full six-year term in the Senate. He was born a slave. When the Civil War broke out, his master took Blanche with him when he went off to join the Confederate army. The slave boy ran away. After the war he went to Mississippi and became a farmer. In 1874 he was chosen to be a senator from Mississippi, but when he went to Washington, the other senator from that state, a white man, refused to introduce Bruce to the Senate. A senator from New York took him by the arm and led him to his place.

Robert Brown Elliott, a representative from South Carolina, had been educated at the best private schools in England. Elliott looked the way most white people thought a black man should look. He was dark-skinned with thick curly black hair.

Pinckney Benton Stewart Pinchback provided people with another problem. He did not look the way most people thought a black man should look. Pinchback had light skin and straight hair. He always said he was black. He said he was black when he was elected state senator in Louisiana and when he became lieutenant governor and governor of Louisiana. People forgot that black people had been in the United States for hundreds of years, living and working with white people. By this time there were many who had both white and black relatives. Pinchback's father was a white plantation owner and his mother was a slave. Major Pinchback and the slave girl, Eliza, whom he freed, had nine other children.

When Major Pinchback died, Eliza was afraid that the major's relatives would try to make her and her children slaves again. She and the children ran away north to Cincinnati, Ohio. Since there was no money now to help bring up the children, Pinckney had to go to work. When he was twelve he became a cabin boy on a canalboat. There were bigger boats around — up and down the Mississippi River chugged the great paddlewheel steamers. Pinckney was a cabin boy and then a steward on one of these. He learned to play cards and he became a riverboat gambler.

During the war Pinckney worked in New Orleans, helping to recruit black soldiers for the Northern armies. After the war he was elected to more offices than any other black politician. Although he was elected to the United States Senate, Pinchback was never allowed to take his seat. For three years the Senate argued about his election. When the senators stopped arguing, they said no to Pinchback.

Congress and Black Men's Rights

Radical Republicans continued to fight for the black men's rights in Washington, but Congress could understand only political rights. Black men should not be slaves. Black men should be able to vote. Congress passed many laws to make sure that they had these rights. The Thirteenth Amendment said no more slavery. The Fourteenth said Negroes should be citizens. The Fifteenth forbade any state to deny anyone the right to vote on the grounds of "race, color or previous condition of servitude." In 1870 and 1871 Congress passed laws imposing heavy penalties for violation of the Fourteenth and Fifteenth Amendments. It was also in 1871 that congressional elections were put under the control of the federal authorities.

What Sumner and Stevens and the other Radical Republicans could not do was to get Congress to give land to the ex-slaves. They could not convince the men in Congress that freedom without some way of making a living was useless. They were strong leaders but they could not move Congress. No forty acres and a mule were to be given to black men.

Both Sumner and Stevens were dying men. Stevens died in 1868. Sumner lived until 1874, dreaming to the end of success for his civil rights bill.

Expansion of the North

One of the problems of the men who were trying to get Congress to do something about the South was that so many things were happening in the North that it was hard for Northerners to pay very much attention to any other place. After all, they had fought the war. Many felt that the Civil War had settled the problem of the South. The time had come for other things.

Many Northerners were concerned with the West. In 1862 Congress had passed the Homestead Act. There were other ways of getting cheap land — states sold land cheaply; railroads wanted people to come west and therefore helped them to buy land. New Englanders and New Yorkers packed their families and their plows into covered wagons and headed west. Settlers came from Europe too. Germans, Swedes, Norwegians, and Danes headed west. Kansas, Nebraska, and the Dakotas began to fill with people.

Some black men joined the westward movement. Some went out

Trains carried settlers westward.

Covered wagons carried settlers to the West.

west as cowboys. Black regiments were sent west to fight Indians. Many of the soldiers stayed on as settlers.

Railroad building took the attention of men all over the country. The Civil War was the first war in which troops went into battle by train. As soon as the war ended, men went to work building railroads all up and down New England and out to Chicago through New York and Pennsylvania. Between 1865 and 1873, more than 30,000 miles of track were laid. By 1880 there were 93,000 miles of railroads in the United States. The most exciting was the railroad that crossed the whole country. In 1869 the last spike was driven in the Union Pacific. Now anyone could ride the rails clear across the United States.

Congress was involved in all this building. Most congressmen thought that railroads were good for the country. New settlers rode the trains and farmers sent their crops to market more quickly. All kinds of goods — pins and plows, coal and calico — moved more quickly to the people who needed them. Congress gave free land to railroad companies, lent money to help them build, and passed laws to make it easier for them to do business. Many congressmen also found that they could get rich themselves by helping their friends who owned railroads.

Farmers were not the only people moving out west. Miners and prospectors found gold and silver in California, Nevada, and the Black Hills of Dakota. Cattlemen found there was a lot of land out west that still was not fenced in. There they could fatten their herds. Cowboys drove the herds of cattle to the West. Dodge City began as a trading post where buffalo hunters could buy their supplies but soon it was full of cowboys bringing cattle to the railroad. The cowboys and the buffalo hunters were both wild men — twenty-five people were murdered during Dodge City's first winter.

New York was the largest city in the land.

Cowboys came to town for a holiday.

Other towns were growing. Before the Civil War most of the factories and large cities in the United States were in the East. Now Chicago was a big city and iron and steel mills were built in Ohio and Illinois.

For a few years after the Civil War many people in the North were making money — farmers, factory owners, workers, railroad companies. Suddenly, in 1873, things began to go wrong. There was a depression. Five thousand businesses failed that year. By the next year three million men were out of work. Farmers had to sell their grain for less than it cost to grow.

Freedom Road

For a few years white men and black men tried to work together. There were never enough white men willing to try, and there was never enough money around for the South to be truly rebuilt. Legislators in Washington never quite understood. The Freedmen's Bureau was never given enough money or enough men to do its job of helping white and black live together. After seven years Congress wearied of the whole idea — and the bureau went out of existence. Reconstruction governments found they could not collect enough taxes to pay their bills. A freedmen's bank was set up to help ex-slaves save and borrow money. Bad luck followed. The bank collapsed in the depression of 1873 that affected business all over the country.

The South was full of ex-soldiers — men who had come back from the war to find their farms and plantations in ruins. When they could not find jobs, it was easy to blame the ex-slaves for their troubles and to feel that if the black man were back in his "place" their problems would be solved.

The first meeting of the Ku Klux Klan was held in Nashville, Tennessee. The leader was Nathan Bedford Forrest, an ex-Confederate general. Soon the members of the Klan were riding out at night wearing white sheets and masks, partly as a disguise, partly to make themselves look frightening. Klansmen whipped black men who tried to vote, burned their houses, hanged black men who defied them. There were other organizations like this — the Knights of the White Camellia, the Red Shirts, the White League.

Whatever the name, these organizations had one purpose — to frighten black men so that they would not vote or try to hold on to power. Those who tried to vote were run out of town or shot.

State governments and the federal government passed laws against such organizations, but nothing could stop them.

Black men who voted the "wrong way" found that they could not get jobs. They, their wives, and their children were threatened. A black father told how his little daughter was killed. She was nine years old and was baby-sitting with a white baby. When the mother came home she could not find her baby's cap. The baby's father beat the baby-sitter so badly that she died eight days later.

A doctor would not come when a black family was sick. The local storekeeper refused to serve black families.

Men were stopped from voting in many ways. There was no secret ballot. Anyone could see how a man voted — and could threaten him or bribe him to vote the right way. Polling places were hidden so that black men would not know where to vote. White

Members of the Ku Klux Klan wore strange costumes to frighten their victims and disguise themselves.

men were allowed to vote many times or to cross over state lines to a place where more Democratic votes were needed.

Black men and the whites who worked with them voted Republican. The Democratic party led the fight to overthrow the Reconstruction governments. Democrats led the fight for white supremacy.

Gradually more and more Democrats came back to positions of power. In 1872 Congress said that Southerners no longer had to swear loyalty to the Union to hold office. Soon all but six hundred Confederate officials were fully pardoned.

By 1869 white men again ruled Tennessee. In 1870 Virginia, North Carolina, and Georgia had all-white governments. Alabama, Arkansas and Texas had no more black men in their statehouses by 1874. In 1875 Mississippi elected an all-white government.

The attempt at Reconstruction, the attempt for black and white men to run the South together was almost over. By 1876 only South Carolina, Louisiana, and Florida were still ruled by black and white Republicans. These governments were kept in power only because there were federal troops there. And 1876 was a presidential election year.

The Election of 1876

The United States was one hundred years old, but many people were not happy with the way the country was being run. White Southerners were angry because there were still federal troops stationed in parts of the South. They wanted to run their states without interference from Washington. Black people were angry because they could see their freedom disappearing.

Many people in the North were angry with the government in Washington. Ulysses S. Grant was a great general; as president he made many mistakes. Everybody always thought Grant was an honest man. His friends, however, often seemed to be making money in ways that were not quite honest. His private secretary was accused of being part of a "whiskey ring" which had helped whiskey manufacturers to avoid paying taxes. Grant's secretary of war had to resign when it was found that he and his wife were being paid $6,000 a year by a man whom they had helped to get a job.

The whole country seemed to be full of politicians who had found ways of getting rich. Samuel J. Tilden, governor of New York, had made a name for himself fighting dishonest politicians in New York

A cartoonist showed Grant and his friends drinking while the handwriting on the wall reminded them of the anger of the voters.

A Democratic campaign poster.   *A Republican campaign poster.*

City. The Democrats nominated him for president. They felt he would get the Southern vote and the vote of those people in the North who wanted honest government.

The Republicans nominated Rutherford B. Hayes, who had fought in the Civil War. The Republicans talked about "Liberty and Union" and did not talk about rich politicians.

In the South, white men continued to threaten black men. A leader in Louisiana said: "We shall carry the next election if we have to ride saddle deep in blood to do it."

In the little town of Hamburg, South Carolina, there was a Fourth of July parade in 1876. Black soldiers paraded. Several of them were arrested for blocking traffic. A mob of white men moved into town to see that the blacks were found guilty. There was a fight and many blacks were killed.

A cartoonist in a Northern newspaper shows a United States soldier protecting a black man from a white Southerner.

When the presidential election was over the vote was so close that no one was sure whether Tilden or Hayes had won. Republicans and Democrats each accused the other of cheating. A special commission of five senators, five representatives, and five supreme court justices was set up to decide who had won the election.

The Republican and Democratic politicians got together and made a secret deal. The Democrats agreed to give up and let the Republican Hayes become president if he would agree to take all federal troops out of the South. Democrats would be able to run the South the way they wanted.

The Republicans agreed — Hayes became president. As soon as he was sworn in he made good his promise. In 1877 all federal troops were recalled from the South. Reconstruction was over.

The End of Reconstruction

When President Hayes brought back the last federal troops from the South he did not have to worry that the United States would split again into two countries. There was still bitterness. Southern families still remembered how Northern soldiers had burned their homes and barns. Families in both the North and the South remembered their sons and fathers who had died in battle. But the white citizens of the North and South had learned how to live together. Never again would they divide into two separate countries. North and South would still argue — but in Congress.

Why then did the people of the South want the federal troops to leave? Partly because they felt it was insulting to have federal troops controlling them. They wanted to run their own lives again.

There was another reason. Federal troops were there to protect the ex-slaves. Southern whites had learned to live with Yankees. They had not learned to live with free black people.

In the years after 1877 the Southern states were able to pass the kind of laws that had made the Radical Republicans so furious in 1866. Black men were kept from voting by special taxes and tests. Separate schools were set up for black children. Black people were not allowed to eat in the same restaurants as whites. They were not even allowed to drink from the same drinking fountains.

One Southern state after another passed these laws. Black people were almost as badly off as they had been when they were slaves. Most of the laws lasted for almost a hundred years.

The black congressmen came home from Washington and stayed. There would be no more black congressmen from the South. The black legislators came home from the state capitals too. All the statehouses would soon have only white members. There would be no more black policemen or black sheriffs or black postmasters in the South — not for a very long time.

It was not quite slavery. Black people had known a few years of freedom. They had set up their churches, their schools, their colleges. Those were not taken away. Black families had a chance to fight together for their future. That they would not give up. The churches continued. Black people worked for white people all week. On Sundays they sang together about freedom. The black schools were poor and shabby. The colleges could not get the money they needed for books or equipment. But they continued. Families scrimped and saved to send their sons and daughters to college, to make them into ministers and teachers and doctors and lawyers. After all their years of schooling, the ministers would go back to their people, to comfort them and give them hope for the future. The teachers would teach in the shabby schools. The black doctors usually could not work in white hospitals — so they worked hard at keeping black people alive. The black lawyers argued in white courts for black freedom. They did not begin to win the argument for almost a hundred years — but they kept on arguing.

While white men had been rebuilding this nation, black men had also used the years of Reconstruction to build. They had built a society of their own — a black society of families and churches and schools which helped them to survive the years of suffering that lay ahead.

Index

African Methodist Episcopal Church, 29
Armies, Northern and Southern, 3-6, 8, 14, 15, 20
Assets in Civil War, North vs. South, 5

Black Codes, 33
Black people
  churches of, 29
  before Civil War, 6-10
  in Congress, 47-50, 62, 63
  family units, 21, 23
  as freedmen, 20-23, 23-28
  occupations of, 6-8, 44
  population, 7
  in Reconstruction governments, 44-47
  restrictions on, 6-9, 33
  rights of, 50, 51
  as slaves, 3, 4, 6-10, 50, 51
Bruce, Blanche K., 48, 49

Carpetbaggers, 47
Churches, black, 29
Civil rights bill, 40, 51
Civil War, 3-6, 10, 12, 15, 32-34
Compensation, Lincoln's plan for, 25
Confederate States of America, 5, 10, 12
Constitution, amendments to, 33, 40, 42, 50

Davis, Jefferson, 5, 11, 20, 48
Debates in Congress, 11, 12, 35, 62
Democratic party, 10, 11, 30-35, 57, 60
Depression of 1873, 55
Devastation caused by Civil War, 14-20
Discrimination, 7, 33, 34, 56, 62, 63
Douglass, Frederick, 9, 10, 11

Education, after Civil War, 23, 27, 28, 45, 46, 62

Elliott, Robert Brown, 49
Emancipation Proclamation, 7, 8

Farms, Southern, 6, 19, 23, 24-26
Fifteenth Amendment, 50
Fisk Jubilee Singers, 28
Fisk University, 28
Food shortages, 15, 19
Forrest, Nathan Bedford, 56
Fourteenth Amendment, 40, 42
Freedmen, 23-28
Freedmen's Bureau, 26-28, 55

Governments, Reconstruction, 45-47
Grant, Ulysses S., 43, 58, 59

Hampton Institute, 28
Hayes, Rutherford B., 60-62
Homestead Act, 24, 25, 51

Johnson, Andrew, 13, 14
   impeachment of, 42, 43
   as President, 30-35, 40-43

Ku Klux Klan, growth of, 56

Lincoln, Abraham, 5, 7, 9, 10,
   12-14, 23, 25, 30, 32

Military governors in South, 20
Money, value of, 20

North, expansion in, 51-55

Pinchback, Pinckney Benton Stewart,
   44, 45, 49, 50

Population, before Civil War, 5

Railroads, 17, 53
Reconstruction
   beginning of, 5, 6
   end of, 61-63
Reconstruction, Joint Committee on,
   35, 40
Reconstruction plans, Lincoln's,
   12, 13
Red Shirts, 56
Refugees, Freedmen and Abandoned
   Lands, Bureau of, 26
Republican party, 10, 11, 60, 61
Republicans, Radical, 35, 36-43, 50,
   62
Revels, Hiram R., 48
Riots, 33, 34

Sharecropping, 25, 26
Slavery, 3, 4, 6-10, 50, 51
Soldiers, return of, 14-20
Stevens, Thaddeus, 36, 38, 51
Sumner, Charles, 38, 39, 51

Taxes, 55, 62
Thirteenth Amendment, 33, 50
Tilden, Samuel J., 59-61
Transportation, after Civil War, 17,
   19, 40

Voting rights, 56, 57, 62

Wade, "Bluff Ben," 39
West, growth of the, 51-55
White Camellia, 56
White League, 56

65

Date Due			
NOV 7 '77			
FEB 13 '79			
NOV 15			
APR 7 '82			
APR 5 '84			
DEC 2 '86			
MAY 15 '89			

4186

973.8   Levenson, Dorothy
L   Reconstruction

Shrine of the Little Flower School Library
Baltimore, Maryland